How Hidden Verses Cast Light

Avishek Rakshit

Qurate
quratebooks.com

HOW HIDDEN VERSES CAST LIGHT

Avishek Rakshit

Published in 2024

© Published by

Qurate Books Pvt. Ltd.
Goa 403523, India
www.qurratebooks.com
Tel: 1800-210-6527, Email: info@quratebooks.com

ISBN: 978-93-58984-89-7

1

The Book of Tobit

Chapter 1: The Exile

And there was a man of Nineveh, a stranger, Tobit, captive with the king of Ninevah, Sennacherib. His name was Tobit; he was an Israelite exiled out of the land of Israel. He belonged to the tribe of Naphtali. He was a pious and righteous man who behaved according to the Torah and all commandments of Moses. He would perform many deeds of charity and conceal the body of a slain Israelite even when the king had ordered that the body of such a killed Israelite be left to be eaten by birds and animals.

Anna and their son Tobias were the constant companions and strength of Tobit. Anna was a wise and caring woman, standing by her husband in all his ways, while Tobias had developed, being a young man of great moral character, forming in the principles and examples given to him by his father.

As he was burying a dead man, Tobit himself became ceremonially unclean and, utterly exhausted, he collapsed and lay down under the wall of the courtyard. And as he slept, sparrow droppings settled warm upon his eyes, and he became blind. This tested Tobit's faith and fortitude; it brought him to despair. Anna went to work to provide for her family, but Tobit, considering himself a burden, prayed fervently for death.

Chapter 2: The Invisible Hand

In the same city of Ecbatana, away from Nineveh, there lived also a woman named Sarah, the daughter of Raguel, who was tormented by the demon, Asmodeus, who slew seven of her husbands on their wedding night, leaving her with desperate great sorrow and disgrace. Just like Tobit, Sarah prayed to die, for she could not take her pain anymore.

Fearing that they would share the same fate, God, through an angel who was named Raphael, sent an angel to Tobit and Sarah to help them. He went in the disguise of a man to Nineveh and found Tobias, who, ignorant of his true identity, took him for the man he was, an Israelite, and even sought to use him as a guide on his way to Media, to retrieve money from the house of a titled relative, Gabael, which Tobit had left usefully with him.

Chapter 3: Departure

It is because Tobit, being unaware of the identity of his guide to be divine, handed the boy named Tobias to the stranger, sending him with the consent "to get the things back in the name of Gabael" and requested his kinspeople to give him a wife. Tobias left his way with his father's blessings and a big bundle of responsibility under the guidance of Raphael.

Walking along, the angel and the boy reached the Tigris River, and a big fish leaped out of it, opening its mouth to gobble up the boy. At his urgent plea, the boy captured the fish and removed its heart, liver, and gall and set them aside, explaining that they would be put to use soon in curing ills.

"These are useful organs," continued Raphael. "The heart and liver drive away demons, and the gall bladder cures blindness."

Cascata saluted from a distance, and Tobias, curious but unsuspecting, carried the fish organs on into Serenbe. These mundane objects he could not have suspected would soon prove so important.

Chapter 4: The Healing Touch

By journeying on with Tobias and Raphael all the way to Ecbatana, they made Raguel, the girl's father, believe that he was a kinsman. Raguel took Tobias, with his servant and his pack, for a kinsman, and he stayed for at least two weeks; thereby they could see their daughter in the house. When he found out about Sarah's situation, he was resolute in saving her, and insuring that she was.

Although Raguel was afraid of the demon Asmodeus, he accepted them with the desire that Tobias would be the one to uncurse Sarah. This night of marriage, as directed by Raphael, Tobias burnt the heart and liver of the fish. This time, the smoke of the fish made Asmodeus flee, the demon that Raphael followed, caught, and tied Asmodeus no more to pass again to harm Sarah.

And the demon was bound to the furthest part of Egypt. After that Tobias and Sarah prayed that God would save them, and they were saved. Now the old man and his wife were in great ecstasy and thanked God for the happiness of their daughter and for her marriage with such nobleman.

Chapter 5: Reunion

After the marriage banquet, Tobias went to collect the money from Gabael, in the company of Raphael. Now they were back with the fortune of bank notes and the great fortune of Tobias's fresh marriage in Nineveh. Lamentably, Gabael was there to rejoice at his return with others, praising God for His bounty.

Now as the couple entered Nineveh, Anna and Tobit rejoiced upon their coming, who, from his coming, had ever been exceeding careful of his return. Their beholding Tobias and his new-married wife abated the general disquiet a little less pinching, though Tobit's blindness hung over them.

On his father's eyes, he placed the gall of the fish, as Rafael had taught him, and he immediately felt that his eyes were filled with pus and aching. Suddenly his eyesight was improved, and Tobit could not thank enough and gave glory to the Lord, exalting Him as a merciful and compassionate God for having an angel named Rafael aid them.

Chapter 6: The Revelation

It was then that Raphael showed his real identity. He told Tobit and Tobias that he was on a divine mission, in fact, one of the seven angels who stand before the Lord. Thereupon, the fear for Tobit, Tobias, and the family increased. They felt awed and reverent in the presence of an angel.

These were the words of Raphael, and they were meant to remind of the unwavering watchfulness and compassion God showed. He saw the ordeal that Tobit and Sarah went through and was the very one who delivered them through his messenger. He even desired them to put their accounts down in writing, for generations to come to realize the mercy and demonstrated manifestation of their faith.

With the mission accomplished, Raphael returned to heaven. Tobit and his family were left to live in peace and spend the rest of life there. Now an old man, Tobit resumed his works of charity and devotion; his faith was even stronger.

Chapter 7: The Legacy

And over the years, Tobias and Sarah got a family on their own. They handed over the teachings from their parents and Raphael, the teachings on faith and trust on the purpose of God. The parents talked about the radiant of resilience and importance of trusting God's will, though sometimes it may not be seen.

The tale of Tobias spread all over the land, inspiring everyone. The narrative was deeply felt among people undergoing similar testing of their own piousness, tribulations, and miraculous healing. It was a testament to the power of faith and the unseen hand of divine providence.

For, indeed, the Book of Tobit got recorded and preserved and passed down generations as a guiding light of hope. The story all over again reminded that, even in the darkest times, the light of God still managed to shine through, guiding and fighting on His own.

Chapter 8: The Message, Everlasting

The saga of Tobit and his family was to be a source of inspiration for believers through the centuries. It reminded them once again that this was a matter of suffering not being forsaken, but a part of the road to understanding and ultimately salvation. Tobit's faith, shown in the event of this blindness and despair, demonstrated how faith in God could lead to results that are completely unexpected and miraculous.

Sarah's story, too, brought out the might of resilience and the liberation from burdens that seemed insurmountable. Her eventual happiness with Tobias underlined the belief in the view that even against the darkest forces, love wins and faith wins. As the Book of Tobit went on to form part of the canon of holy scripture, the lesson of the book was doubled in sermons, prayers, and daily living. The story announced that there were angels among humanity, unseen, but always ready to aid and serve. The story encouraged humans to be faithful in times of adversity, to do good, and to rely on that plan, a plan of God's which, through how it will play out, is not obvious. The legacy of Tobit and his family remained a fire, therefore, a true perennial witness of the sustaining power of faith, love, and divine providence. That is the light that shone through their story, recorded and shared through the ages; it shines still to light the way for those seeking hope and assurance in their own journeys.

2

The Book Of Enoch

Up in the ancient world, before the rise of empires and the spread of civilizations, lived a man by the name of Enoch–a patriarch, a prophet, and a scribe whose life and visions would be chronicled in the Book of Enoch. This text, non-canonical, is venerated by some; others find it to be the most controversial. It gives a peek into the celestial realms in between and the mysteries of the divine.

He was the grandfather of Noah, a man who walked with God; he did not taste of death in the way that the common man does. He was taken to the heavens and given visions and knowledge that would illuminate that which so many generations forward would not have. His canon, which was placed in the Book of Enoch, is an account of his divine experiences, prophecy, and teachings.

It all began with the story of the Watchers, a legion of angels whom God had charged with watching over the affairs of mankind.

At one time, two hundred members of this group of Watchers descended from the pinnacle of Mount Hermon to Earth. They were captivated by the allure of human women and contravened the divine order by marrying them. From this union came a race of giants called the Nephilim. This giant size and strength helped them to further the havoc and ruin on Earth, extracting vast resources from it in the advancement of violence and corruption.

The Watchers introduced the knowledge that was forbidden to the men, such as the secrets of heaven. Having been in a process of corruption themselves, they corrupted men and developed into further decadence. Azazel as the leader of the chief Watchers taught the men 'to make swords and knives, shields, and breastplates.' He taught them metallurgy of secrets. Their leader Semjaza taught enchantments and root-cuttings. This knowledge will be propagated and bear extreme wickedness and the contamination of the Earth.

It was an inheritance of this message–that God's judgment was to be delivered by Enoch, God's elect representative. Through a dream, he was transported to the ends of the earth, where he saw a waste howling in utter darkness and fierce fire. It was here that he was made to see the Watchers, shackled and bundled up until the final Day of Judgment. He was to deliver God's word of their final doom: the Watchers and their offspring, the Nephilim, would be cut down, just like their corrupt oversight of God's creation.

Enoch found himself traveling not only to celestial realms but also to the remotest corners of the earth. He saw the secrets of the universe, the movement of heavenly bodies, and machineries of creation. Set upon by the angels, Enoch moved between the realms of light and darkness and secured insight into divine order. And so he wrote down his visions–like a tapestry woven by the finest thread of detail—giving the world cosmology and telling in full all the mysteries of the heavens and the earth.

The deepest among the Book of Enoch's part is the "Astronomical Book" or the "Book of the Celestial Bodies." In it, he describes in detail how the cosmos works, sandwiching the cycles of the Sun, Moon, and Stars in between. He explains to us the Moon's phases, determination of the seasons, and the calendar. He ascribed their activity to the divine order set up by God. Enoch's descriptions show deep knowledge in astronomy, blending scientific observation with theological insight.

In another vision, Enoch is conveyed into the heavenly sanctuary and beholds the glory of God and His angelic hosts. He saw in the vision the great throne of God with hosts of angels in the court, each having a definite office in the divine order. This increased the grandeur and magnificence of the vision, but Enoch felt it to be a reinforcement of his sense of purpose and mission. A scroll is handed to him containing knowledge and wisdom to be given to humanity, a record of his office as a divine scribe.

The Book of Enoch contains prophecies of the coming judgment and the future of humankind. Enoch prophesies about the Great Flood, divine intervention meant to cleanse the earth of its corruption. He prophesied the consequence of wickedness, clamored for repentance, and called on the people into righteousness or adherence to divine law. He even continued with prophecies past the flood in which the coming of the Messiah and a new era of peace and justice will be enjoined.

Of all the Book of Enoch, the most interesting segment is the "Book of Parables," where Enoch sees visions on the "Son of Man"—this is `that which is messianic´—who shall bring about salvation and judgment. The Son of Man is a self-qualifying heavenly being, radiated on his throne of glory, overseeing things in the final judgment. It's a vision underlined with double themes of hope and accountability, with a promise of redemption upon the righteous and retribution to the wicked.

The teachings of Enoch are wisdom and understanding. He calls every man to seek knowledge and live in the ways the divine principles propose. In fact, the writings are full of exhortation to righteousness, warning one of the snares of sin, and encouragement to a way of living in virtue. The writings of Enoch, either in wisdom or those divine encounters that lit his way, are that torch of light for man in the nettlesome ways of life.

This influence is not confined to these early days; he is influential in the perceptions of later religious expressions, such as early Christianity and Judaism. The state of the fallen angels, conditions relating to the Nephilim, the final judgment–a great deal of the implications of these subjects–sound forth through scriptural texts and theological writings. The role taken on by Enoch as a prophet and scribe, the visions of heavenly realms, and a call to righteousness set the die for religious conceptualization and the literary tradition followed by him.

The Book of Enoch also dwells on the moral and ethical aspects of human life. The visions of Enoch disclose the results of human activity and importance of dealing justly, leading to the necessity for atonement. He speaks about corruption pervading humanity and how divine intervention is needed in order to restore order. Deeply critical to human behavior, his writings call for a turning back to righteousness and adherence to divine law.

The story of Enoch testifies more than that about transforming characteristics, previously victorious in divine encounters. His ascent into heaven, visions of celestial worlds, and appointment as the divine messenger give evidence that the human being may rise above the limitations of the earth. Such an experience as that of Enoch reinforces in human beings the conviction of deep mysteries beyond the visible world and communion with the divine.

In the Book of Enoch, at the end, one gets a vision of the final judgment and setting of a new heaven and earth. In it, Enoch sees the righteous receive eternal life, whereas the wicked are thrown into the abyss. Thus, the great vision really points to the themes of accountability and hope that course through the text as a glimpse into the greatest fulfillment of God's plan for humanity.

The Book of Enoch is quite special among the religious writings because it accompanies itself with a testimony toward divine mysteries. The text is woven into a rich tapestry of insight that continuously acts as an inspiration to and a challenge on the readers, integrating cosmology, prophecy, and moral teaching. Enoch's journey, from being a patriarch to a celestial scribe—with his visions of the heavenly realms and his teachings on righteousness and wisdom—compares with few others as a timeless account of the quest for understanding and the pursuit of virtue. The Book of Enoch is represented as an invitation to reflect on the enigma of existence, the mantra of divine justice, and the possibilities transformations extend through divine encounters. Enoch's story of mingling celestial and earthly realms takes a profound plunge into human nature and the tenacity of the search for truth and meaning. Visions and teachings of Enoch enjoin us to wisdom, righteousness, and a deeper understanding of that divine order inwrapping the universe. The themes of the Book of

Enoch that this paper reflects upon include the enigma of existence, the mantras of divine justice, and the transformation extended by divine encounters, and celestial delight mingled with earthly sorrows in the story of Enoch. His visions and teaching called for wisdom, righteousness, and an understanding of divine order. In the twilight of his life, Enoch's legacy speaks of a beacon of light in the midst of a wildly chaotic world. His writings inscribed into the Book of Enoch continue to speak of the deepest longings of the human heart and in such a way give access into wisdom, understanding, and union with their divine. May the insight of Enoch direct one in harmony with divine principles that structure this very cosmos, and may it direct in the actualization of the full potential of human beings made in the image of God as we undertake our earthly pilgrimage. Indeed, the story of Enoch, from the Book of Enoch, is one that has no time; eternally, it longs to be a true tale of divine wisdom that changes human lives and man's quest for knowledge. His visions, prophecies, and teachings are the treasure that gives one inspiration and challenges until today. And when one thinks of the travels of this man, he realizes that beyond this earthly realm lies the unseen great mysteries and the potential of the divine. Enoch teaches mankind three things: to generate wisdom, to walk in the path of rights, and to seek into the divine order undergirding all creations.

3

The Letter of Clement to James: A Tale of Ancient Wisdom and Apostolic Succession

In the busy center of ancient Jerusalem, inside the city walls, the air was full of the smell of spices and the hum of voices in bargaining. It was a time for the early Christian community to grow; amidst that noisy sound, the apostles were spreaders of the teachings of Jesus. This is where our story began, with an epistle that would become the testament of faith, wisdom, and the conservation of sacred teachings.

Chapter 1: The Call to Leadership

And the very important task was given to Clement. His mentor and master, Peter, knew, from a premonition that bad days were on the horizon and in order to keep their message alive and spread, a great and able leader was needed. So, he sent a letter to James, brother of Jesus, as he had become the head of the Church in Jerusalem.

Out of all humanity, there was the choice of Clement to bring this momentous letter, being among the humble but intellectual around. He left for Jerusalem, carrying the scroll and knowing very well what lay ahead of him. A walk to Jerusalem is never easy, but his will spur him on and on.

Chapter 2: Arrival in Jerusalem

Having come to Jerusalem, the first Christian congregation received Clement with open arms. He was brought to the very humble James, who had nevertheless much respect, almost authority, in that congregation. Upon his arrival, he saw James sitting with deep problems in his eyes and a quiet manner, which was exuding wisdom that was commanding and yet soft.

Handing it over in a sort of awe, Clement realized that the message inside the scroll was a key to the future of their faith. James nodded graciously after taking the scroll out of Clement's hands, immediately realizing the significance of the message on that piece of parchment. The room was instantly hushed momentarily as James unrolled the parchment and began to read under his breath the words contained therein.

Chapter 3: The Message

"Brother James, bishop of bishops, peace be with you." The reed Peter's words into the letter indicated a tone both warmly pressing. He remained completely faithful to James' guidance and his critical role of leadership in steering the young church through its critical, developmental stage.

In the teachings passed on by Jesus, Peter tells us how he had believed it important that the purity of His teaching be kept. Peter speaks of the hardships both without and of the contentions encountered among one another within the community. Peter seemed quite concerned that the doctor be preserved and went on to caution James to be on the lookout lest he be deceived by those who would seek to pervert what Jesus had taught him.

Succession Leadership was also raised in the letter. Peter, realizing that he was practically at the point of martyrdom, asks James to make due provisions that the leadership positions be taken over by men of spritely spirit. The leaders should not only be spiritually but doctrinally competent.

Chapter 4: The Burden of Responsibility

As James read, a feeling of being loaded down came over him. This was no easy task ahead, but he felt fortified because of the heavenly guidance given him by Jesus and the Holy Spirit. He realized that under his leadership the saving of their teachings and their church unity had been preserved.

The fact is that there was a meeting among the apostles and elders in response to the letter of Peter. It was a very serious gathering, and everybody knew about the seriousness of their mission. James spoke about the words of Peter, and together they thought of the best way forward to ensure continuity and purity of faith.

The debates were intense; there were opinions counter opinions. Some argued for it to be understood very liberally to embrace all opinions; others insisted the original teachings be understood literally. James was very attentive to these lectures, meditating over every point.

Chapter 5: Unity In Diversity

The purpose of James was to devise an answer, in the wisdom that he knows, that would balance doctrinal purity with the diversified experiences that they were beginning to go through. He repeated the issue of unity and love, reminding them all that the very nucleus of Jesus' message was compassion and inclusiveness.

He was not recommending that the essential doctrines were to be changed; rather, these ought to be left with no room but the possibility of interpretation and dialogue. James' attitude was to be liberal and to lean more on a church powerful in doctrine yet merciful in demeanor.

The apostles and elders, realizing that the suggestion that was given by James was quite wise, consented to his wise counsel. They concluded to gather a presbytery that would take care of the doctrine matters by making sure that any variation was set right by general consultations. The presbytery would be the same organ to give guidance on the appointment of more leaders to ensure that the doctrine was preserved through their teaching.

Chapter 6: The Legacy of Leadership

Then, with the council set, James went on to appoint leaders who were in possession of the virtues of faith, wisdom, and humility. Clement was one of the enigmatic figures whom James appointed to be members of this illustrious group since Clement had dedicated his life to the workings of the mind. The infant church blossomed under James' leadership. The teachings of Jesus were held in reverence, and there was steady growth within the strength of faith in the community. Indeed, Peter's letter had become a cherished document in the mind of the one who came across this reminder of that sacred trust that had been passed down through the apostles.

With inspired form this deep wisdom that he had practically seen, experienced, and learned he kept on serving with unabated devotion. He wrote, for the posterity of the sacred journey, the events and teachings of the early church.

Chapter 7: Trials and Tribulations

With the years came their triumphs and trials. Their faith, upon which persecutions so early came, was not to be shaken. Guided by the unwavering hand of James and armed with his wisdom and compassion, turmoil could be met with solace and strength.

The great trouble was the erroneous teachings that almost broke up the church. James, with all the rebukes of Peter fresh in his memory, called the council to order. Correct speech and much patience allayed the disputes and brought peace.

The rumor about James being a wise and just leader had reached well beyond the Christian community, and even those outside had learned of him and came to him for advice. His way of combining severity with tenderness was what won respect for him from his followers and adversaries alike.

Chapter 8 Passing the Torch

James reached the age and passed on the leadership. He called Clement whom he then trusted, now an Elder, to continue the work they had begun. He accepted, humbled by the trust put in him, with the solemn vow to uphold the teachings of Jesus.

James, in his final days, wrote a letter to Clement, almost in a manner similar to that Peter had done to him. He passed on the teachings, his blessings, and the faith into the future in his sight: Clement. The letter was a testimony of the chain of wisdom and leadership since Jesus had passed it on to the apostles.

Chapter 9: Clement's Journey

With the death of James, Clement assumed the leadership as his personal responsibility. He carried on with the teaching and history of the church, so that the legacy of the early church would not be lost. Very valuable, therefore, did his writings turn out to be for the future generations, as much as the infusion of wisdom from Peter and James.

Under the leadership of Clement, the spirit of inclusiveness and intellectual rigor was presented well. He encouraged the formation of communities that questioned and explored faith with reason and dialogue. It was under his leadership that the early church survived and served to preach and spread the word of God around the world.

Chapter 10: The Enduring Legacy

The letter of Clement to James and the events that followed would come to stand as the hallmark of Christian tradition; a story of faith and resilience, wisdom passed from one generation to the other. The early Christians, in their trials and triumphs, laid the foundation of faith that would stand pole to pole through millenniums.

The writing of Clement–survivors now, kept as treasures–gives a diminutive light of their life, struggle, and success of the early church. They are to be reminded of the sacred trust that had been committed to them: a trust demanding twin virtues of faithfulness to its teaching and compassion to its practice.

Epilogue: A Testament of Faith

Even in history, a letter of Clement to James will take its place among the documents to the eternal strength of faith and wisdom in benign governance. Really, this is the story that inspires: the one about strength to be found in unity and wisdom that comes from humility and devotion. Through their unwavering commitment, early Christians secured the teachings of Jesus for posterity. Their legacy includes love, wisdom, and an unbroken strand of faith that has steered and fostered millions around the globe and will continue to do so. Therefore, Clement's letter to James is a source of hope, and it calls to mind that sacred trust in those who lead and teach. This is a story, though set in ancient days, that yet repeats of old the eternal message regarding faith, wisdom, and the enduring power of the human spirit.

4
The Acts of Peter

It was in this sprawling city of Rome in the first century that a wave of change rippled through its ancient streets. And so it was that the story of Peter, the humble fisherman from Galilee that many said was to become the most pivotal identity in early Christianity, would come to be called the Acts of Peter.

Peter, originally named Simon, was an average fisherman who lived and worked by the Sea of Galilee among the common people of that region. His transformation began when he was being called by Jesus of Nazareth to be an apostle and "fisher of men." His name was changed to Peter, meaning "rock"; he became one of the most intimate disciples of Jesus. After the crucifixion and resurrection of Jesus, Peter became the leader of the small Christian community.

The Acts of Peter really date from Jerusalem, where he was filled with the Holy Spirit and preached Jesus' message boldly. His words touched many but at the same time incited huge anger in the Jewish authorities and Roman officials. He was often beaten, thrown to jail, and threatened, but nothing could impair his faith. Miracles began to follow him, not for the sake of miracles but also as a kind of evidence of the divine character of his mission.

One such outstanding miracle took place in Joppa. There lived a disciple named Tabitha, whose Greek name was Dorcas. She was a very good person, who did many good things for the poor and gave a lot in charity. She fell sick and died; and her body was washed and laid in an upper room. Since Lydda was near Joppa, the disciples, hearing that Peter was in Lydda, sent two men to him to urge him, "Please come to us without delay." So Peter set out and went with them. The disciples in Joppa received him in the upper room, where all the widows stood by him weeping, showing the tunics and other garments that Dorcas made while she was with them. But Peter put them all outside, knelt down, and prayed; then turning to the body he said, "Tabitha, get up." She opened her eyes, and seeing Peter she sat.

Peter soon made his way to Caesarea, where an important vision awaited him—an event that would change the course of his ministry. In a trance, he beheld a great sheet coming down from heaven, full of all manner of beasts. A voice told him to kill and eat; being a good Jew, he refused, citing the dietary laws. The voice said to him, "Do not consider anything impure that God has cleaned up." This happened three times, and Peter was at a loss for what it could possibly mean. The message dawned on him when he got a call to go to the house of a man called Cornelius, a Roman centurion and a Gentile. Peter went into the house of Cornelius and preached the gospel to them, even though he was loath to do so; and Cornelius and his household were converted and baptized. This marks the turning point, a great sign indicating that the message of Jesus was meant for all humanity and not specifically for the Jews.

Yet this new mission of Peter's among the Gentiles was not unopposed. Jewish believers in Jerusalem called Peter and upbraided him for having gone to eat with the uncircumcised Gentiles. Peter thereupon told them of his vision, and of the outpouring of the Holy Spirit upon the household of Cornelius, to show that in this action his critics were silenced and the universality of the gospel was proven.

Peter grew in influence, but the dangers that surrounded him increased. It so chanced that King Herod Agrippa, in order to make himself popular with the Jews, began a violent official attack on the new faith. James, the brother of John, was put to death with the sword, and Peter was arrested and thrown into prison. The night before he was to be brought to trial, Peter was roughly awakened from his sleep by a blow on the side. The chains fell off his wrists. He was guided out beyond the first and the second watch by an angel of God. Peter, though, thought he was seeing a vision, as he realized that he was free only after the angel left him. He went to the house of Mary, the mother of John Mark, where many people had gathered and were praying.

But Peter continued on his mission, visited the regions to gin up the Christian communities, and afterward he was in Rome, the epicenter of the Roman Empire. It was a city of mixed cultures, ideas, and religions, constituting the ideal soil for Christianity thrusts but also marked by high danger. This could not have remained unnoticed by many in Rome, where he was destined to be one of the important members of the Christian community. Peter was able to comfort and reassure the believers. With the authority he was gaining, though, he had less comfort for the authorities, and especially for the devilish Nero, a fierce persecutor of the Christians.

Perhaps one of the most fantastic tales in the Acts of Peter is that of a sorcerer called Simon Magus, who had entranced the people of Samaria with his magical arts. Simon, or Simon the Magician, was in fact also baptized, but not with honest intentions. He was observing the apostles, who, after baptizing believers in Samaria, laid their hands on their heads so that they would receive the Holy Spirit. Anyway, it was Simon Magus that came to the apostles who did that, and he offered them money in order that he may gain the power of the Holy Spirit to pass it on to other people. And Peter said directly to him: "Your money perish with you because you have thought that the gift of God may be obtained with money." Simon Magus begged for forgiveness, and although the story provides no information of what happened to him from that time on, his story has become an example of the difference between true faith and mere sorcery.

Simon's and Peter's path would cross again in Rome. Simon had endeared himself to Nero. By his claims of using magic, he was considered a court magician. Simon claimed that he could fly. He showed many different magical feats. He was brought before a crowd, which included Peter, who bowed into prayer that God may show the people that Simon was a liar. Simon jumped off the tower, and contrary to his claims, he crashed into the ground. His bones were smashed, and his two legs were broken. He was brought out as a fraud.

This incident strengthened the reputation of Peter more than anything else, but it made Nero resent him all the more. The emperor considered Peter a danger to his power and the order of the empire. The Christian community, which was under a bad plight anyway, was now increasingly getting persecuted.

Amid all this, Peter had his vision—soon to be one of the most potent episodes in his story—of Jesus walking in and about the city. Peter said, "Lord, whither art thou going?" The Lord answered, "I go to Rome to be crucified afresh." Peter knew his duty and returned to the city, facing his destiny with a strong display of resolve.

Peter was very quickly seized and sentenced to death. His last wish was to be crucified upside-down, since he did not feel fit enough to be killed in the same way as Jesus. And this last wish came true on the part of the authorities: Peter died with dignity and faith, leaving a colossal legacy that inspired and inspired generations of Christians.

Not only are the Acts of Peter sequels of one another, but they also testify to faith, the high potential of the human spirit, and the transforming ability of divine intervention. Peter's life was transformed from being a mere poor fisherman into one of the leading pillars of the Christian faith through his sheer bravery, commitment, and unflinching dedication to his higher calling. His life and actions became the basis for so much of the early church's developing doctrines and practices. The miracles he performed, the sermons he preached, and the sacrifices he made allowed for the spread of Christianity beyond the Roman Empire. To this day, the Acts of Peter is such a powerful combination of miraculous events and deep teaching on faith and devotion. As the story of Peter has been continually told and retold, it serves to remind us of the indomitable strength of belief and the impact that one man can have upon the course of history. His legacy lives in millions of hearts—a true testimony to the timeless message of hope, redemption, and an unyielding pursuit of truth.

5

The Gospel Of Judas

Chapter 1: Discover

In the arid deserts of Egypt, near the ancient city of Thebes, an archaeological team made a shocking discovery. Among the ruined walls of a forgotten monastery, inside a sealed clay jar, lay hidden a collection of papyrus manuscripts. These texts, fragile and brittle from centuries of neglect, looked unlike any other that the archaeologists had experienced; they were written in the unmistakable markings of Coptic script, a language used by early Egyptian Christians.

Right at the front of the dig was Dr. Miriam Donovan, a world-renowned archaeologist and early Christian text expert. As her workers salvaged and preserved the writings, Dr. Donovan's excitement grew. Then there it was, among them all: "The Gospel of Judas," stated its title in the faint ink of its time.

The discovery caused a ripple not only in scholarly circles and other religious groups but even in popular media. Indeed, the Gospel of Judas was among those texts lost, with the very knowledge of its existence known through references in early Church fathers' writings. After nearly two millennia, now the manuscript had reemerged, promising to shed the new light on one of the most enigmatic figures of history.

Chapter 2: The Tale of the Betr

The process of deciphering and translating the text was initiated by Dr. Donovan, her team, and first-class conservators. The perspective provided by the Gospel of Judas was remarkably dissimilar from that of those works that had been canonized in the New Testament. Rather than being the worst traitor, in this biblical text, Judas was even singled out by Jesus for a very special, highly controversial assignment.

The Gospel of Judas casts Jesus in a light where he trusted Judas with the knowledge of mysteries of the cosmos and the true nature of God; this was a being far-removed from the wrathful deity many believed in. In private conversations, Jesus revealed that there had to be a betrayer, and Judas was to play this role in a different sense, without malice, for some higher purpose.

The text represented the material world, the world of pure spirit living, and to this world, Jesus attempted to restore humanity. In this gospel of Gospels, Judas was not a traitor but was a wonderful instrument to accomplish Jesus's work. By his own willpower of giving away, Jesus made competent enough to move all and sundry regarding the crucifixion and resultant resurrection to save humanity.

Chapter 3: The Academic's Dilemma

The implications for the Gospel of Judas were vast, and at the same time, it was controversial. Dr. Donovan was in a very delicate position. She was extremely worried about possible reactions from religious communities that might consider the text heretical. Yet, being a scholar, she was committed to revealing and sharing the truth, no matter how challenging that would be.

Dr. Donovan then took her results and presented them at an international congress focusing on texts of early Christianity. The reaction was immediate and polarized. The discovery was hailed as innovative by some scholars, giving new dimension to the understanding of early Christianity, while for others it was decried as forgery or dangerous heresy.

While this debate was going on, Dr. Donovan was taken aback by an uninvited guest. Intent on his mission, Father Gabriel Rossi is a Jesuit priest whose specialization deals with church history. Believing in an open mind about theology and all matters of dispute associated with it, he had an interest in the manuscript as according to his point of view, accepting divergent perspectives might help in shedding light on faith and thus be able to portray better the events about which that very faith revolves.

Together, Dr. Donovan and Father Rossi try to recreate the history and theology of Gospel of Judas; analysis that will be very imposing to bring about diversity and cohesion with the other thoughts of early Christianity.

Chapter 4: The Hidden Context

As he and Father Rossi start reading from the manuscript, even Dr. Donovan himself is taken aback by the larger meaning he finds within the text: a Gospel of Judas written in this violent controversy of early Christianity, with multiple beliefs and interpretations trying to emerge from the melee.

The text testifies to aspects of Gnostic thought itself: the belief in an esoteric knowledge and differentiation between two elements–whatever is material and whatever is spiritual. The Gnostics thought this life was the misbegotten work of the demiurge creator god; the real God was outside this world. They believed that one could achieve salvation only through awareness and actualization of the Divine Light within.

In this context, the Gospel of Judas portrayed Jesus as a revealer of hidden knowledge towards which Judas was guided. This redemptive scenario opposed the orthodox views that prevailed in early Christian doctrine and presented another way to spiritual liberation.

Both Dr. Donovan and Father Rossi saw in the Gospel of Judas something more than historical curiosity: they saw a window into the diversity of early Christian beliefs. A great opportunity was there to develop dialogue and come to an understanding between two different faith traditions, based on compassion and openness in theological discussions.

Chapter 5: Revelation

The scholar and father prepared to present their new findings to an expectant audience at a symposium that had called theologians, scholars, and representatives of religious communities at large together to discuss the meaning of the Gospel of Judas.

It was a symposium held in one of the most prestigious universities with a lot of mainstream media coverage. The feel inside the hall was one of both expectation and calmness. While Dr. Donovan delivered her translation and explanation of the document, she concentrated on the need to actually have an open-minded approach towards such documents and situations mentioning that early Christianity has a wide variety of thoughts.

Father Rossi followed with the theologian's perspective. He showed them how important it is to know different histories, and how much its knowledge may bring about growth. Continuing, he said they should look at the Gospel of Judas not as a threat to their faith but more as an invitation into the exploration of the faith itself.

The discussion was thus heated and varied in its comment. Some of them, however, found a deep disagreement with the text, seeing it almost as a direct challenge to their doctrines, but others even saw some value in that alternative viewpoint for such purposes as deepening the insight into early Christian history.

Chapter 6: The Aftermath

The public disclosure of the Gospel of Judas had two-edged results for both the academia and the religious world. It raised a lot of controversies but also led to increased research on early Christianity, other traditions it had and the newly discovered materials that could throw more light on this era that shaped much faith. This interest of scholars got directed towards other non-canonical writings of the same relevance for the nascent period of the faith.

For Dr. Donovan, this was to prove a defining moment for her career. Subsequently, through her research, she helped contribute to an even more comprehensive body of knowledge about early Christian literature. Her work made scholars across disciplines work together and, consequently, created a more inclusive and dynamic academic community. Father Rossi's role in the symposium drew part accolades and part affronts. Part of the church seemed to take his openness to other texts as under controversy, yet part of it appreciated his role in the symposium–showing dialogue and understanding. He became an advocate for interfaith discussions, promoting a message of unity and compassion.

Chapter 7: Heritage

A once-lost-to-history Gospel of Judas took on new, one-of-a-kind significance in early Christianity. That reminder to believers of the intricate multilateral nature of their faith is always a challenge to open up to the richness of their own traditions while being open to new perspectives. The work of Dr. Donovan and Father Rossi inspired a generation that burgeoned with inquiries by scholars and theologians on the fusions of history, faith, and culture. Their work drew attention on the need of preservation and studies in ancient texts where even those most controversial contributed to, in each manuscript, the need of knowing more about human search for truth of things. The debate and interpretation of the Gospel of Judas continued, but it also became an icon in the search for truth and knowledge. This book again reminded humanity that history is not a single unchanging narrative but a tapestry woven from many threads, each in itself contributing to the richness and complexity of the whole. In the end, the Gospel of Judas was not a story of betrayal but rather a testament to the force of discovery, dialogue, and understanding. It was such a tale that rose above the years and taught all who would read to find beneath the surface and seek deeper truths than that which merely met the eyes.

6

The Wisdom Of King Solomon

In the golden age of Israel, when the kingdom was at its zenith, King Solomon ruled with unrivaled wisdom and prosperity. His reign, marked by peace and grandeur, became the epitome of a ruler blessed with divine insights. Among his many contributions, the Book of Wisdom became one of the strongest testimonies of his deep and profound understanding of life, virtue, and divinity.

Solomon, the son of King David and Bathsheba, came to the throne of Israel in his early years as a result of divine intervention. It was at this time that he felt the severity of his duties and developed a great sense of responsibility and humility. It can be remembered that it was in a dream that God approached him, ready to offer anything that Solomon would wish. And since he realized the gravity of the role that had been assigned to him, he asked for wisdom to be able to guide the people with justice. Pleased with Solomon's request, God did grant him unmatched wisdom along with a wealth and honor beyond measure.

The base of Solomon's reign was divine wisdom—the decisions, the verdicts, and the way of inculcating the people—all of it was underlaid by insights beyond human understanding. Following the book ascribed to Solomon, The Wisdom of Solomon, whose author intertwines practical advice with deep theological reflections, unfolds his considerations. Opening with the pursuit of wisdom and righteousness, Solomon propounds wisdom as a divine gift and served to those who desire it earnestly. He juxtaposes the ways of the rightly self-controlled and the sinner as though illustrating the ultimate victory of the virtue over the vice. "Love righteousness, you rulers of the earth," he sums up for the rulers, an exhortation towards strict integrity and justice.

The reflections of Solomon on wisdom become closely intertwined with his understanding of the divine. He interprets wisdom as something to do with the revelation of God's nearness, a guiding light, and a signpost leading toward a life of goodness and meaning. He writes that "For wisdom is more mobile than any motion; because of her pureness she pervades and penetrates all things," drawing attention to the inclusive and transformative character of wisdom.

In the final analysis of his thought, Solomon proves the existence of divine wisdom by the beauty of creation. The diversity and harmony in the entire natural world, in its very nature, reflect the fingers of its Creator. Solomon is taken by the beauty in the harmony of creation and in its representing divine wisdom in so many ways. He extols the miracle of Heaven, the regular times and the seasons, the delicate balance between life forms—everything attests to wisdom immanent and at the same time transcendent.

A considerable part of the Book of Wisdom is devoted to the subject of justice, that of the righteous and of the wicked. Be assured, Solomon calms down his readers, justice will be done at last, though it may seem that it is lagging. Suffering of the righteous and success of the wicked is transient; divine judgment will eventually be fair and sure. "But the souls of the righteous are in the hand of God, and no torment will ever touch them," he consoles and encourages those who suffer for righteousness' sake.

The Wisdom of Solomon is addressed to practical discernment in living a good life. He sets himself against envy, pride, and greed, but he calls for humility, generosity, and modesty. His wisdom reflects deep insight into human nature, with its strengths and frailties, and a compassionate urge to lead his people towards a life of fulfillment and peace. He said, "Wisdom is a kindly spirit," urging his readers to embrace those virtues that will lead to harmony and well-being.

Perhaps the most fascinating aspect of the Book of Wisdom is the exploration undertaken by Solomon into the human condition and the pursuit of immortality. He comments on the brevity of life and the certainty of death, themes that must be close to the human heart. Still, Solomon speaks with hope and transcendence. He speaks of the soul's immortality and the eternal reward for the righteous. "The righteous live forever, and their reward is with the Lord," he assures, giving an outlook on life that transcends earthly living.

Solomon's wisdom also comes from his understanding of leadership and governance. He writes of the qualities of a just ruler, speaking mainly of wisdom, justice, and compassion. According to Solomon, a good leader is one that humbly serves and seeks the welfare of his people above personal gain. He speaks again from his own experiences as rank, a king, having to cope with the intricacies of running state machinery and the attending responsibilities that power brings.

The Book of Wisdom also probes deeply into the mysteries of God's providence and the role of suffering in His divine plan. Solomon reflects and tries to answer why the just should suffer and the wicked prosper. He offers a nuanced view, acknowledging the limitations of human understanding while affirming the ultimate goodness and justice of God. Suffering, he suggests, can be a means of purification and growth, leading to a deeper reliance on divine wisdom.

Solomon's reflections on wisdom do not remain within the abstract principles; they are personal and experiential. He narrates his own struggle for and acquisition of wisdom, presenting his life as the witness to the transfigurative power of divine discernment. Humility and reverence are integral aspects of Solomon's writings, for he knows that wisdom is essentially a gift from God, never the fruit of human knowledge.

The wisdom of Solomon is a legacy that transcends his reign and the boundaries of Israel. His teachings left an indelible impact on the following generations, moulding the morality and spirituality of Western man. Timeless are the insights and deep the reflections of the Book of Wisdom, which never ceased to inspire and instruct those who strive to live a life of virtue and knowledge.

As Solomon's glorious reign continued, his wisdom was sought by many leaders and scholars. The Queen of Sheba, having heard about the glory of Solomon's reign and his matchless wisdom, visited Jerusalem to test him with hard questions. In response, Solomon solved all the problems she put before him so easily that she was amazed at the depth of his comprehension and the beauty of his court. The visit of the Queen of Sheba attested to the reputation of Solomon as a paragon of wisdom, a man whose name was on the lips of every ruler in the world.

At the same time, the life of Solomon is a warning to all. Even with unparalleled wisdom, he was unable to avoid the dangers of both power and prosperity. Thus did he contract alliances with foreign nations by marriage, and introduced foreign gods and usages into Israel. This had the effect of gradually undermining all the religious zeal which he had shown at the commencement of his life, and, as such, was a very fair proof of the weakness of human nature.

This way, the Book of Wisdom testifies on the one hand to Solomon's superlative wisdom and, on the other, to the fallibility of man. It is knowledge that commands mankind to seek wisdom with the earnestness of one's heart, to live righteously, and to long to learn a deeper understanding of God. The successes and the challenges which Solomon's life bore are a life of the transforming power of the wisdom and the unending quest for truth and virtue.

Ultimately, Solomon's wisdom bequeaths to humanity through the wisdom literature of this book. It is a deep portrayal of the moral and spiritual spheres of life, giving hope and inspiration for a walk in accord with divine precepts. Here, Solomon invites us to take the journey of discovery: the pursuit of wisdom with humility and holiness; the seeking of the virtues that make a fulfilled and peaceful life.

As one thinks about the Wisdom of Solomon, it comes over one that his teachings are for all time. His connection between the nature of wisdom, justice, and the human condition remains one that is coherent across time, offering that light of hope in the darkness that so often pervades this world. Solomon's legacy, therefore, lives on in the Book of Wisdom, inspiring and guiding those who wish to lead a life of integrity, compassion, and understanding.

In his latter days, Solomon looked back over his life with a sense of fulfillment and–strange as a word for him–humility. He had been given incomparable wisdom, riches, and honor in this world, but he saw that true magnanimity lay in doing right and fearing the Lord. The Book of Wisdom bears witness to his lifelong quest for wisdom and care to make what he had conceived in mind known to the future generations.

Besides, since we read the world through the eyes of Solomon's wisdom, we see the beauty and order of creation. We note the divine presence manifesting in each and every manifestation. It tells us to live humbly, to practice justice, and to be proficient in the virtues that will give us a life of harmony and happiness.

The Book of Wisdom of Solomon is a very practical book in its teachings and very theological in its reflections. It is never out of date. It meets the inmost needs of the human heart, pointing the way in all truth and wisdom. We walk through life led by the wisdom of Solomon's insight, seeking wisdom with humility, living within the harmony of divine principles that rule the celestial bodies and guide him.

And so the story of Solomon and his wisdom rings down the ages like a torch that lights its place in a world too often dimmed by darkness. His wisdom, written in the Book of Wisdom, continues to inspire and guide, giving timeless testament to the power of divine insight into an endless search for truth and virtue. In his very words, let us set out on this learning expedition, inquiring with all earnestness and humility for wisdom and in a life that reveals truths and beauty as in the remainder of the world divinely ordered.

Among the epic tales, the wisdom of Solomon truly epitomizes the transforming might of divine insight and eternal thirst for knowledge in the history

Starting action

The Wisdom of Solomon: A Retelling

In the golden age of Israel, when the kingdom was at its zenith, King Solomon reigned with unmatched wisdom and prosperity. His reign, marked with peace and grandeur, had actually come to be synonymous with the rule of divine insight. Among the many gifts he had ever given to men was the Book of Wisdom, known by many names, including the Wisdom of Solomon.

Solomon, belonging to the very few lucky sons of the great King David and Bathsheba, took over the reigns of Israel at a very young age. He was much of a man of great responsibility but, at the same time, also a man of great humility. One night, God came to him in a dream and asked him to desire something. Knowing the enormity of the task which has been assigned to him, Solomon wished for wisdom, since he needed it to be a good king to his people. God liked his request and, with it, gifted Solomon with unmatchable wisdom, along with wealth and honor that others could not compare to.

It was this divine wisdom that Solomon based his reign upon. His very decisions, judgments, and teachings were filled with an insight unknown to the common populace. The Book of Wisdom, therefore, is supposedly written by Solomon but is also a cocktail of these teachings, both practical and deeply theological. The book begins with a prayer on the pursuit of righteousness and a meditation on the nature of wisdom. Solomon notes in this section that wisdom is a divine gift, accessible to all that ask for it with sincerity of heart. He then goes on to compare the paths of the right and the wickedness, noting the ultimate success of vice over virtue. "Love righteousness, you rulers of the earth," he declares, asking of leaders to govern with integrity and justice.

Solomon's reflections on wisdom are deeply interwoven with his understanding of the divine. He sees wisdom as an outworking of God's nearness, a beacon that guides toward a life of goodness and delight. Writing, "For wisdom is more mobile than any motion; because of her pureness she pervades and penetrates all things," he reiterates the fact that wisdom, in its activeness, reaches out to encompass everything and effect deep change.

Most of the time, in his moments of reflection, Solomon looks upon the magnificence of creation as an expression of divine wisdom. Everything in the natural world, with its complexity and beauty, signals the touch of the Creator. In these situations, Solomon is awed at the creation, the orderliness, the balance of things, aspects of situations in which he sees a divine model of intelligence. He praises the heavens, the orderly seasons, the delicate balancing of life, all of which are evidence of wisdom that is both here and far beyond.

A large part of the Book of Wisdom continues on the theme of justice, especially in relation to the just and the evil. Solomon takes time to convince his readers that divine justice is inevitable even though not realized immediately. The sufferings of the just and seeming advantages of the wicked are temporary, for God's judgment will ultimately be just and sure. He writes, "But the souls of the righteous are in the hand of God, and no torment will ever touch them," thus offering hope and solace to those who will persevere suffering for the sake of righteousness.

On a more practical level, Solomon's wisdom is more concrete, more sound advice on how to live. He inveighs against envy, pride, and greed and praises humility, generosity, and moderation. His teachings speak clearly of an understanding of human nature with all its strengths and weaknesses and demonstrate compassion, urging his readers to lead lives with virtues that result in accord and well-being.

One of the most attractive features of the Book of Wisdom is Solomon's effort to scrutinize the human situation and the search for immortality. He muses over the shortness of life and the death that is for sure. These are themes that are very close to the human experience, but Solomon writes about a life of hope and worth that transcends flavors. He speaks of the immortality of the soul and the enduring gift for those who are good. "The just live forever, and in the Lord is their recompense," notes the author, giving an impression of life that goes far beyond life on earth.

One also finds Solomon's wisdom in his comprehension of leadership and governance. He offers advice on the virtues of a just prince that include wisdom, justice, and compassion. A good king, in the view of Solomon, is one who rules with some sense of humility, serving the interest of his people. His thoughts on leadership were not only theoretical but raised from his very own life experiences as a king, dealing with the challenges of governance and the management of power.

The Book of Wisdom also delves into the mysteries of God's providence and the mystery associated with suffering in the divine plan. Solomon is observed to attempt to address the oldest question of why the just suffer while the wicked flourish. He gives a balanced view, acknowledging man's limitations in understanding yet affirming God's ultimate goodness and justice. Through suffering, he suggests, one may come to experience purification and growth toward a greater dependence on divine wisdom.

Solomon's thoughts about wisdom don't stop with abstract musings but are eminently personal and very practical. He speaks of his own odyssey of both seeking and obtaining wisdom, and his life is a witness to the transforming power of divine insight. All of Solomon's writings come with a sense of humility and reverence, for he well understood that true wisdom was a gift from God, never to be obtained by humankind.

The impact of Solomon's wisdom went beyond his land, Israel, beyond the centuries which separated him from modernity. His teachings have touched the lives of many generations, shaping the moral and spiritual worlds of people who call themselves Westerners. The Book of Wisdom remains to be a source of inspiration and light for those who think of living a life of virtue and wisdom.

In later years of his reign, the wisdom of Solomon was sought after by the world's leaders and scholars. The Queen of Sheba, hearing of Solomon's wisdom and wealth, went to Jerusalem to test him with difficult questions. But when she arrived, she questioned Solomon on every subject in her mind. Tremendously successful, Solomon answered all of her questions with startling insight, dazzling her with his answers and his court. The Queen of Sheba's visit wasn't entirely a diplomatic one, however. It well served also to confirm Solomon's reputation as a wise, God-fearing king to whom all other kings looked with respect.

But the story of Solomon serves as much for inspiration as it does for example. Even with innumerable wisdom at his disposal, he was not to escape the insidious traps of power and prosperity. It was in these later years that he established alliances through marriage with foreign nations, and in so doing, brought the gods and practices of these nations into Israel. These things served to show how even the wisest of men can have his earlier faithfulness to God whittled away a little at a time.

The Book of Wisdom is, thus, a record of both Solomon's breathtaking brilliance and his life's depiction of the complexities of human life. It admonishes readers to seek wisdom in all earnestness, to live righteously, and to seek to know more from the divine. Therefore, the life of Solomon is in its ups and downs–how wisdom transforms and how there is a perennial quest for truth and virtue.

At the end, therefore, Solomon's wisdom, rolled in the Book of Wisdom, is a gift to humanity. It is the gift of understanding the depth of moral and spiritual involvements of men's lives, to help and inspire them to take a walk in accord with divine laws. Solomon, through his writing, thus calls us on a journey of discovery, to seek wisdom with humility and awe, and walk in the way of virtues that lead to fulfillment and peace.

More so, upon reflection about the Wisdom of Solomon, the timelessness of the teaching continues to remain evident. On the one hand, the Wisdom of Solomon regarding the kind of human beings who bear the best value and the best choice shines across time and space like a great beacon illuminating the world full of darkness. The legacy of Solomon, as enshrined in the Book of Wisdom, continues to inspire and guide those who desire to live life with integrity, compassion, and understanding.

As Solomon's life and reign drew to a close, he looked back with fulfillment and humility—blessed with an unequalled measure of wisdom, wealth, and honor—still able to fully respect that genuine greatness was not in such things, but in the pursuit of righteousness and the fear of the Lord. The Book of Wisdom is a standing record of his persevering quest for understanding and the necessity of sharing with others the input of the experiences he had gained.

Following Solomon's example, one is invited to look afresh at the world, not just in reevaluation of the beauty and order of creation but with a vision of the divine presence that surrounds everything. We are to live lives of humility, of justice, and of other virtues from which a harmonious and fulfilling life results. In these ways, the Book of Wisdom combines sound practical advice with profound theological reflections in a treasure that speaks to the very heart of humanity and shows the way to true wisdom and insight.

Let this be the story—Solomon and his wisdom in a world that shines evermore, a light in too dark of a world. It will continue to inspire and will lead, for its teaching is ever enshrined in Wisdom's book, which is a perpetual monument to divine insight and to the unending search for truth and virtue. He says he called us to the journey of our own discovery, to seek wisdom in all seriousness and humility, and to live a life of beauty and order of the divine. The wisdom of Solomon in the records of history was an illustrious and very powerful divine power to insight and the lasting endeavor to understand. Found within the Book of Wisdom, these teachings remain the guide of the time for anyone desiring to live a life of integrity, compassion, and purpose. Through his life and wisdom, one is reminded how much impact a single man's search for truth and virtue carries into the world and inspired toward their journey of self-discovery, bearing in mind that the light of divine wisdom will serve as their guide.

7

The Gospel Of Thomas

Chapter 1: The Discovery

In the musty repository of an old monastery, lost in the hills of Syria, a remarkable discovery was made. It was 1945, and an adventurous team of archaeologists, led by Dr. Eleanor Carter, had been searching through the ruins of some of the earliest Christian communities. They had been hunting for unknown manuscripts, squirreled away for centuries, with the possibility to yield new insights into the origins of Christianity.

Amid the parchment and papyrus fragments emerged the outline of one manuscript–a book of sayings attributed to Jesus. In Coptic, it carried the provocative title, "The Gospel of Thomas." The document bore little resemblance to the large, sprawling accounts of the Gospels in the New Testament. This was simply

114 sayings, or logia, attributed to Jesus—many of them completely new to the scholars.

In the hands of Dr. Carter, a professional archaeologist and scholar of early Christian writings, it was immediately clear what this would mean. The Gospel of Thomas was going to prove an invaluable source into the research of the teachings of Jesus; it may give new evidence to some of the earliest unfolding of Christian spirituality. The document was taken to a conservation laboratory, where it would be cleaned and assessed through a series of delicate conservation steps.

Chapter 2: The Scholar's Hunt

In order to translate and interpret the manuscript, there were required a whole team of linguists, historians, and theologians. She calls upon Father Daniel Moreau, a Jesuit priest in whom a great interest in Christian mysticism has been kindled. Together, they started the long and careful translation of the ancient manuscript.

In the course of their work on the manuscript, they began to discern the nature of what Jesus's teaching was. The Gospel of Thomas focused on the inner enlightenment and self-discovery of every person, and the happening of the divine happens directly via personal experience. Many of the sayings were so cryptic that it challenged the reader to be able to dig deeper. For instance, one of the sayings mentioned, "The kingdom of God is within you and all around you. Split a piece of wood, and I am there. Lift up the stone, and you will find me." The idea of the divine happening directly through personal experience and the immanence of God reached out to Dr. Carter and Father Moreau's hearts, which made them interested and concerned about the origin and implications of the text.

Chapter 3: The Hidden Wisdom

The Gospel of Thomas was found to have its roots in the mystical traditions of early Christianity, stemming mainly from Gnosticism. Gnostic scriptures often dealt with the hidden knowledge (gnosis) and the concept that eternal life comes to those who have the knowledge of their true divine selves.

Dr. Carter and Moreau evaluated the role of the Gospel of Thomas between its relation with other early Christian writings. The parallels were seen with the Nag Hammadi library, a place in Egypt from where Gnostic texts were excavated in 1945. Hence, the Gospel of Thomas had its relation to a philosophical strain that moved within early Christianity and valued individuality's spiritual perception rather than dogma or regulation.

The text also questioned the traditional view of Jesus as just a miracle worker and a savior; rather, he was portrayed as a wisdom teacher, guiding his people toward self-realization and the understanding of the divine in all things. The image opened up heated discussions among scholars, which forced them to reconsider long-accepted ideas about the historical Jesus and the diversity of early Christian thought.

Chapter 4: The Public Disclosure

As the translation was nearing completion, Dr. Carter and Father Moreau were preparing to bring their discovery to the public.

They organized the meeting at the University of Paris with scholars, theologians, and representatives of different religious communities to consider the possible consequences of the Gospel of Thomas.

The event was given a lot of attention by the press. All were talking about the possible potential that the newly discovered text had in bringing a positive change. The expectation and curiosity made the atmosphere in the room electric when Dr. Carter took the stage to start with the introduction to the translation and interpretation of the sayings. For the beginning, she told about its essential role in the highlighting of inner enlightenment and the way it may contribute to the enhancement of contemporary practice.

Father Moreau continued with theological reflection, stating that the issues of the Gospel of Thomas' correspondence to the mystical traditions endemic to not only Christianity but other world religions. He urged the readers to have an open mind when reading, as it will help them realize Jesus' teaching in the most profound sense and benefit their spiritual life.

The discussion at the table was lively and diverse. Some of the participants greeted the Gospel of Thomas as a valuable supplementation to Christian usage. Others had suspicions about its authenticity and theologies. Nevertheless, there was the general feeling that seized everyone, surprise regarding the abundance and plurality of early Christian thought.

Chapter 5: The Impact of Modern Spirituality

The Gospel of Thomas eventually appeared in the public domain, which led to long-term repercussions not only in academic but also among religious circles. Scholars continued to read the text, trying to find parallels with other early Christian literature and to find the significance of the document for the history of religion.

Nowadays, to many spiritual seekers, the Gospel of Thomas was a different Jesus teaching. Emphasis on the inner discovery and direct experience of God found a chord with those, who want to make spirituality more individual and more experience oriented. Study groups and retreats, aiming at understanding the value of the Gospel of Thomas, became more and more popular. Renewed attraction to the early Christian mysticism has grown exponentially.

In this way, Dr. Carter and Father Moreau agreed. Interfaith dialogues - by these dialogues, the quest for inner enlightenment and the immanence of divinity became known to the followers of different religious movements. The dialogues were able to represent a common path in spiritual comprehension and the approval of the importance of personal experience in the road of faith.

Chapter 6. Scholar's Journey

Finding the Gospel of Thomas became a milestone in Dr. Carter's life. She continued her academic research, incorporating the knowledge to the general understanding of early Christian writing. Her research also provided the opportunity for many scholars from other fields to unite and create an open and dynamic scholarly society.

The involvement of Father Moreau in this academic research also became crucial for his future ministry. He began promoting mystical and contemplative practices in contemporary Christianity, offering everyone unity and mercy. His attempts to make the religious establishment pay attention to contemporary spirituality also became successful. He and Dr. Carter published a book about the Gospel of Thomas; the book was able to present the historical context of the document's creation, theology issues, and the influence it had on contemporary spiritual life. The success of that work proved extraordinary and placed them among the best scholars in the field of early Christian studies.

Chapter 7: The Legacy

The lost Gospel of Thomas was, in a sense, found again and had come to occupy its special place in the study of early Christianity. It was a prod to encourage believers to recover the richness of their traditions and, at the same time, to keep their minds open to new ways of looking at human possibilities.

Dr. Carter and Father Moreau had pulled off the work that would bring a new generation of scholars and theologians to dwell on the interface of history, faith, and culture. With their lays, this importance was reinforced–that ancient text be preserved and further explored, but more so, it recognized how each of every manuscript, regardless of how controversial, would lead to further enlightenment in the ever-unfolding record of the human quest for meaning.

The Gospel of Thomas had continued to be the stuff of argument and reargument, but also the icon of the long and deathless quest for knowledge and truth. The tale was made to remind the world that history was not one story but a tapestry woven of many threads, each contributing to the richness and complexity of the whole.

Last but not least, to them, the Gospel of Thomas was not just a collection of sayings but an example of the strength of discovery, dialogue, and understanding. Its story was one that spanned time and asked that anyone, past the façade, seek out the deeper truths that lie underneath.

8

The Bell And The Dragon

Chapter 1: The Arrival

In the center of the ancient kingdom of Elaria, there was the vast city of Viridion, looming dominantly over the entire kingdom with its great towers, occupied markets, and the ground of the majestic castle of King Alden–a city dripping with legend and lore. But, above all of their many wonders, the most loved of all was the Great Bell of Viridion, a stupendous structure that hung in the central plaza, cast in an age long forgotten and enchanted by the most skillful sorcerers throughout the kingdom.

No ordinary bell, it was said that its chimes could be heard around the world, and thus, it could calm the storms, call rain in times of drought, and even reach those most sorrowful in the world.

A beacon, if you will, for the people of Elaria, together in unity and strength. Like all ancient relics, though, it held its secrets close to the chest, and very few could fathom them.

One fateful day, a traveler had come to Viridion. His simple, weather-beaten garb seemed out of place amidst the grandeur of the city, yet there was something strange about him that drew curious eyes among those who passed him by. His name was Seraphin, and he was a wanderer and scholar of the arcane, known in hushed circles for his enormous knowledge and mysteriously darkened past. His entry was no accident; he had come in search of a legend, a tale told in whispers in the darkest corners of ancient texts: the Dragon's Bell. The exact tale of the texts told that the Great Bell of Viridion was made not by human hands, but with the guidance and power of a dragon—a creature of supreme might and wisdom—once flying over the skies of Elaria.

Chapter 2: The Legend

The dragons were the protectors of Elaria; they guarded the lands and people from all potential threats. Drakara was the mightiest and most wise among them, standing not only in his strength but in his understanding of the ancient magics of the world. In their darkest hour, when the kingdom was beset by invasions and natural calamities, he became an ally of the human king ruling at the time. They worked together to forge a plan. They conceived of a bell, which would help harness the dragon's power and protect the kingdom, and so it would from thereon out.

The forging of the bell was no simple matter. Drakara poured a piece of himself into the bell, fusing his soul within the metal.

For as long as the bell continued to exist, so would Drakara, its spirit watchman, on the lookout for the kingdom's well-being and prosperity. But such a bond was not forged without its price: his physical body was no more, the dragon was no more—only his spirit remained a watcher, forever bound to the artifact's fate.

Centuries passed, and the true story of the bell was left in myth, leaving only a legend. The people of Viridion may have known of its powers, but none knew of the dragon's sacrifice. Seraphin, through his relentless quest for knowledge, knew fragments of this truth of old. His path into the temple of Viridion was purposed to complete the knowledge and power of the bell, its nature, and Drakara's bond.

Chapter 3: The Scholar's Quest

Seraphin had sought for an audience with King Alden, who had taken an evident interest in the tales of the man, featuring a scholarly edge to his otherwise adventurous life. The king granted Seraphin audience at the royal archives—a deep trove of knowledge—holding scrolls and tomes from eras of ages long past. For days unending, the magician buried himself in the archives. He now knew of the history of the bell and the dragon. He found that the enchantments of the bell were growing weak, and the bond with Drakara's spirit was fraying. If left unattended, the bell would lose its power, leaving Elaria vulnerable to the whims of fate.

And so, spurred on by this discovery, Seraphin knew something must be done. Without further contemplation, he gathered the required reagents to summon forth the ritual of restoration—the rare and powerful ingredient at hand was that of a dragon tear. Of a dragon's tear, the ancient texts spoke with awe-inspiring usefulness.

It held magical properties of immense importance, capable of enhancing and renewing enchantments of the highest order. But dragons no longer resided in Elaria.

But Seraphin was not to be the one to give up now. He consulted further with the most learned sages and mages in the land. Hidden was said to be a valley, resting in a land of mystery, secret–a place thought to be the last sanctuary of the dragons. And so, armed with this knowledge and with the blessing of King Alden, Seraphin set out on a perilous journey to find this valley. And get the precious tear.

Chapter 4: The Hidden Valley

For the next days, his journey took him across treacherous landscapes, through dense forests, over towering mountains, and desolate arid deserts. Using his knowledge of the arcane, he was guided and able to find his way through magical wards and traps that would keep any other intruder at bay. After weeks of travel, he arrived at the entrance to the hidden valley, a place untouched by time and filled with an otherworldly beauty.

The deeper the valley was, the more potent the aura Seraphin felt. The very air was thick with magic, the very ground seemed to pulse with life independent of everything else. And there, he met Auryn, the last dragon of Elaria. Shining like a starlit sky, his scales luminescent, his eyes a prism of colour as they shone with some ancient knowledge.

Auryn had been guarding the valley and this part of the world's secrets for centuries. He knew of the world beyond but had chosen to remain ensconced in this hidden part of the world. So Seraphin, on his part, told his quest and the situation that had befallen upon Viridion. His own words were full of emotion and told the long tale of Drakara's sacrifice and the need to restore the enchantments of the bell as their only protection for the kingdom. Auryn listened carefully; the sorrow and understanding deep inside the shining eyes were clear for Seraphin to see.

Chapter 5: The Dragon's Tear

Seeing the grief etched in Seraphin's face and the knowledge of Drakara's sacrifice did the work on Auryn. He relented. The dragon cries, in a magical droplet, a drop filled with the essence of his being. Seraphin took it, with a heavy heart but with his full acknowledgment because he knew what this act meant. Once he held the dragon's tear, he knew he must leave Elaria.

Before he left, Auryn gave him one last piece of wisdom; he told him of the balance between power and responsibility. He told him to protect, not with just might; he told him to protect them with wisdom and compassion. Seraphim swore to keep the bond with Drakara alive and to make sure that the knowledge of the bell and the dragons never died away.

Chapter 6: The Ritual

On returning to Viridion, Seraphin could not waste a second. Of course, a key was the dragon's tear, its magic multiplying the spells and restoring the power. More and more, continued the ritual, more and more this Great Bell of Viridion lit in some shining light. The air was vibrant, and the sound of the bell chime touched all the kingdom by its deep melodious tone, replenishing the hearts of all the people with hope and tranquillity. The spirit of Drakara, chosen by the dragon, given a spell through its tear, re-energized by the tear of the dragon, once again, its presence was established in the bell, and its protective powers to remain through the test of time, through the generations.

The Great King Alden and the citizenry of Viridion praised the victory of Seraphin as they redoubled their hope and faith in the Great Bell of Viridion. The kingdom prospered as the people lived amicably and prospered under the shield of the Great Bell.

Chapter 7: Legacy

Seraphin's story did not end with the rejuvenation of the powers of the bell. He continued in his pursuit of knowledge, writing down the things he had learned and the truths that he had found. He went on to establish a new order of scholars and mages, guarding the heritage and magic of Elaria so that the legend of the bell and the dragons could be passed down through the many years ahead.

Auryn remained in the hidden valley, a secret warden to the secrets, silent in the knowledge that his tear kept the kingdom safe. He trusted in Seraphin and his order to respect the balance between power and wisdom that guided Elaria into a future of peace and understanding.

The Great Bell of Viridion continued to chime, its clear song reminding all of the world that man and dragon were forever bonded–that there was sacrifice, but also great opportunity in unyielding unity. Thus passed, to all appearance, the legend of the bell and the dragon, the Indian prince's gift, the tale of magic, of fearlessness, of eternal interwoven locks that bind us all.

9

The Book of Jubilees: The Hidden Chronicles

In a time long ago, lost in the mists of ancient history, there was a sacred text known as the Book of Jubilees. This mysterious manuscript, hidden away and revered, offered a unique retelling of Genesis and Exodus, the foundational books of the Hebrew Bible. It wasn't just a repetition of familiar stories but a chronicle of divine revelation, celestial beings, and the intricate dance of time and destiny.

Chapter 1: The Celestial Decree

As the heavens opened, a divine voice echoed through the cosmos, calling upon the Angel of the Presence. This angel, a radiant being of immense wisdom and power, stood before the Eternal

Throne, ready to receive the celestial decree. "Write down the events of the world," commanded the Almighty, "from the creation of Adam to the exodus of My people from Egypt, and beyond. Let it be known to generations that time is measured and sanctified."

With a quill of light and a scroll of ethereal parchment, the Angel of the Presence began the sacred task. Thus, the Book of Jubilees was conceived, its words filled with divine truth and eternal significance.

Chapter 2: The Creation of the World

In the beginning, the world was a void, a formless expanse of chaos. But the Almighty spoke, and there was light. The first day dawned, and the separation of light from darkness marked the rhythm of time. On the second day, the firmament was fashioned, a vast expanse dividing the waters above from those below.

As days turned to nights and nights into days, the earth took shape. On the third day, the dry land emerged, and vegetation sprouted from its soil. The fourth day saw the creation of the celestial bodies: the sun, moon, and stars, each destined to govern time. On the fifth day, the waters teemed with life, and birds soared through the skies. The sixth day brought forth the animals, and finally, man was created in the image of the Divine.

Adam, the first man, and Eve, his companion, were placed in the Garden of Eden, a paradise of unparalleled beauty. The seventh day was sanctified as the Sabbath, a day of rest and reflection, marking the completion of creation.

Chapter 3: The Fall and the Promise

In the Garden of Eden, Adam and Eve lived in harmony with nature and their Creator. Yet, the serpent, cunning and malevolent, sowed seeds of doubt in Eve's heart. "Did God really say you must not eat from any tree in the garden?" he hissed. Deceived, Eve partook of the forbidden fruit, and Adam followed suit. Their eyes were opened to the knowledge of good and evil, and innocence was lost.

Banished from Eden, Adam and Eve faced a harsh world. But even in exile, there was hope. The Almighty promised redemption through their offspring, a future savior who would crush the serpent's head and restore harmony.

Chapter 4: The Lineage of the Righteous

Generations passed, and the world filled with human life. Among Adam and Eve's descendants were the righteous and the wicked. Cain, consumed by jealousy, slew his brother Abel, marking the first murder. Yet, Seth, another son of Adam, continued the lineage of righteousness.

The descendants of Seth walked with God, while the lineage of Cain spiraled into corruption. The wickedness of mankind grew, and the earth was filled with violence. Yet, among the chaos, there remained a beacon of hope - Enoch, a man who walked with God and was taken up into the heavens without tasting death.

Chapter 5: The Great Flood

The corruption of humanity grieved the heart of the Almighty. Determined to cleanse the earth, God decreed a great flood. Yet, Noah, a righteous man, found favor in the eyes of the Lord. He was instructed to build an ark, a colossal vessel to preserve life.

For forty days and forty nights, the rains fell, and the fountains of the deep burst forth. The earth was submerged, and all life perished, save for Noah, his family, and the creatures within the ark. When the waters receded, a new world emerged, and God established a covenant with Noah, symbolized by the rainbow, a promise never to destroy the earth by flood again.

Chapter 6: The Tower of Babel

In the post-flood world, humanity multiplied and journeyed eastward. They settled in the land of Shinar and, driven by pride, resolved to build a city with a tower reaching the heavens. "Let us make a name for ourselves," they declared, "lest we be scattered across the earth."

But the Almighty descended to witness their creation. Displeased by their arrogance, God confounded their language, causing them to speak in tongues. Unable to communicate, they abandoned their project, and the city was named Babel, for there the Lord confused the language of the world.

Chapter 7: The Call of Abraham

From the lineage of Noah's son Shem arose a man named Terah, who fathered Abram. The Almighty called Abram to leave his homeland and journey to a land that God would show him. "I will make you a great nation," declared the Lord, "and through you, all the families of the earth shall be blessed."

Abram obeyed, embarking on a journey of faith. He wandered through Canaan, where God promised that his descendants would inherit the land. Despite his wife's barrenness, Abram believed in the promise, and his faith was counted as righteousness.

Chapter 8: The Covenant of Circumcision

In his old age, Abram was visited by the Lord and given a new name - Abraham, meaning "father of many nations." God established a covenant with Abraham, marked by the rite of circumcision. "Every male among you shall be circumcised," commanded the Lord, "as a sign of the covenant between Me and you."

Sarah, Abraham's wife, miraculously bore a son, Isaac, in her old age. The promise of countless descendants began to unfold, and the legacy of Abraham was secured.

Chapter 9: The Sacrifice of Isaac

In a test of faith, God commanded Abraham to offer Isaac as a burnt offering. With a heavy heart, Abraham obeyed, journeying to Mount Moriah with his beloved son. As Isaac lay bound on the altar, an angel of the Lord intervened. "Do not lay a hand on the boy," declared the angel, "for now I know that you fear God."

A ram, caught in a thicket, was provided as a substitute sacrifice. This act of obedience solidified the covenant, and the Almighty reiterated the promise of numerous descendants and blessings.

Chapter 10: The Descendants of Abraham

Isaac married Rebekah, and they had twin sons, Esau and Jacob. Though Esau was the elder, Jacob, through cunning and divine providence, secured the birthright and blessing of his father. Fleeing from Esau's wrath, Jacob journeyed to his uncle Laban's house, where he married Leah and Rachel, fathering twelve sons.

Jacob, renamed Israel, became the patriarch of the twelve tribes. His favored son, Joseph, was sold into slavery by his jealous brothers but rose to prominence in Egypt. Through a series of providential events, Joseph saved his family from famine, bringing them to Egypt, where they thrived and multiplied.

Chapter 11: The Bondage in Egypt

The descendants of Jacob, known as the Israelites, prospered in Egypt. However, a new pharaoh arose who feared their growing numbers and enslaved them. The Israelites endured harsh bondage, their cries for deliverance echoing to the heavens.

In the midst of their suffering, a child named Moses was born. Saved from a decree of death, he was raised in Pharaoh's palace. Yet, his heart was with his people. Fleeing to the wilderness after killing an Egyptian, Moses encountered the Almighty in a burning bush. "I have seen the affliction of My people," declared the Lord, "and I will deliver them from bondage."

Chapter 12: The Plagues of Egypt

Moses returned to Egypt, accompanied by his brother Aaron, to confront Pharaoh. "Let My people go," demanded Moses, speaking the words of the Lord. But Pharaoh's heart was hardened, and he refused. Thus, the Almighty unleashed ten devastating plagues upon Egypt, each a demonstration of divine power.

The Nile turned to blood, frogs overran the land, lice and flies tormented the people, and livestock perished. Boils afflicted the Egyptians, hail devastated the crops, locusts consumed what remained, and darkness engulfed the land. The final plague, the death of the firstborn, broke Pharaoh's resolve. He released the Israelites, who departed hastily, their exodus marked by the first Passover.

Chapter 13: The Crossing of the Red Sea

As the Israelites journeyed from Egypt, Pharaoh's heart hardened once more, and he pursued them with his army. Trapped between the Red Sea and Pharaoh's chariots, the Israelites despaired. But Moses, with divine authority, stretched out his staff, and the waters parted. The Israelites crossed on dry ground, while the pursuing Egyptians were swallowed by the returning waters.

This miraculous deliverance became a cornerstone of faith, a testament to the Almighty's power and faithfulness. The Israelites, now free, journeyed to Mount Sinai, where they would receive the law and covenant that would shape their identity.

Chapter 14: The Giving of the Law

At Mount Sinai, the Almighty descended in fire and smoke, the ground trembling at His presence. Moses ascended the mountain to receive the law, inscribed by the finger of God on tablets of stone. The Ten Commandments formed the foundation of this covenant, guiding the Israelites in their relationship with God and with one another.

But the Israelites, in their impatience, fashioned a golden calf and worshiped it. Moses, descending with the tablets, was furious. He shattered the tablets, and the idolaters were punished. Yet, through intercession, Moses secured God's forgiveness, and new tablets were provided.

Chapter 15: The Wilderness Wanderings

The Israelites, led by Moses, journeyed through the wilderness toward the Promised Land. Their path was fraught with trials and tribulations. They faced hunger and thirst, yet the Almighty provided manna from heaven and water from a rock.

Despite witnessing countless miracles, the people grumbled and rebelled. At Kadesh-barnea, their lack of faith led to a devastating decree - they would wander the wilderness for forty years, until a new generation arose. Only Joshua and Caleb, who trusted in the Lord, were promised entry into the Promised Land.

Chapter 16: The Final Victory

As the years of wandering drew to a close, Moses prepared the Israelites for their imminent entry into Canaan. He recounted their journey, the laws, and the covenant, urging them to remain faithful. Moses, unable to enter the land himself, appointed Joshua as his successor.

Moses ascended Mount Nebo, where he beheld the Promised Land from afar. He passed away, and the mantle of leadership fell upon Joshua. Under Joshua's command, the Israelites crossed the Jordan River and commenced the conquest of Canaan. The walls of Jericho fell, and city after city succumbed to their advance.

Chapter 17: The Eternal Promise

With the land secured, the Israelites settled in their inheritance, each tribe receiving its portion. The covenant established with Abraham, reaffirmed through Moses, found fulfillment. Yet, the story of the Book of Jubilees did not end here. It extended beyond the immediate victories and conquests, reaching into the future with promises of eternal significance.

The Book of Jubilees emphasized the sanctification of time, the observance of Sabbaths, and the cycles of jubilees. It foretold the coming of a messianic age, a time of ultimate redemption and restoration. This sacred text, hidden and cherished, remained a testament to the divine orchestration of history and the unwavering faithfulness of the Almighty.

10

The Gospel of Mary Magdalene

Introduction

The Gospel of Mary Magdalene is a gnostic text, one of the many ancient writings that didn't make it into the canonical Bible. This text offers a unique perspective on the teachings of Jesus Christ and emphasizes the role of Mary Magdalene, often considered a key figure in early Christian history. Though discovered in the late 19th century, it wasn't until the mid-20th century that the fragments of this gospel were translated and made widely available. This narrative seeks to illuminate the story contained within these fragments, presenting a compelling and detailed account of Mary Magdalene's spiritual journey and her relationship with Jesus.

Discovery and Significance

The discovery of the Gospel of Mary Magdalene in the sands of Egypt was a significant event in the study of early Christian texts. Found in 1896 as part of the Berlin Codex, the manuscript contained several gnostic works, but it was the Gospel of Mary that drew particular attention. Written in Coptic and Greek, it offered a different lens through which to view the teachings of Jesus, portraying Mary Magdalene not merely as a repentant sinner but as a leading disciple with profound spiritual insights.

The significance of the Gospel lies in its content, which challenges traditional Christian views on authority and gender roles. It presents Mary as a favored disciple, entrusted with deep esoteric teachings by Jesus. Her prominence in this gospel suggests that early Christian communities might have had a more egalitarian structure than later church hierarchies.

The Fragmented Text

The existing text of the Gospel of Mary Magdalene is incomplete, with substantial sections missing. The surviving portions can be divided into several key parts: the dialogue between Mary and the disciples, her vision, and the ensuing discussions. The narrative begins in the middle of a conversation between Jesus and his disciples after his resurrection. Jesus is depicted imparting final teachings before his ultimate departure.

Jesus' Teachings on the Nature of Sin

The gospel opens with Jesus addressing his disciples on the nature of sin and the soul's ascent. He emphasizes that sin is not an inherent part of human nature but rather a consequence of actions and ignorance. This teaching diverges from traditional doctrines that view sin as an intrinsic part of the human condition since the Fall of Adam and Eve.

Jesus encourages his disciples to seek within themselves for the path to salvation, highlighting the importance of inner spiritual knowledge over external rituals. This esoteric approach to spirituality is a hallmark of gnostic thought, which emphasizes direct, personal experience of the divine.

Mary's Role as a Spiritual Leader

After Jesus departs, the disciples are left in a state of confusion and fear. They express doubts about their mission and their ability to continue spreading Jesus' teachings without his physical presence. At this critical juncture, Mary Magdalene steps forward, offering reassurance and guidance.

Mary recounts a vision she had of Jesus, in which he revealed to her profound mysteries of the spiritual realm. She speaks of the ascent of the soul, describing stages and barriers that must be overcome to achieve true spiritual liberation. This vision underscores her intimate connection with Jesus and her deep understanding of his teachings.

Mary's vision includes a dialogue with Jesus about the nature of the soul and the obstacles it faces in its journey toward enlightenment. She describes encountering and overcoming entities that personify ignorance and desire, culminating in the soul's ascent to a state of peace and knowledge. This mystical journey reflects gnostic themes of enlightenment and the transcendence of earthly desires.

Conflict and Authority

Mary's recounting of her vision and her authoritative stance stir mixed reactions among the disciples. While some, like Levi, accept her account and her role as a leader, others, notably Peter, challenge her authority. This conflict illustrates the tension within early Christian communities regarding the role of women and the nature of spiritual authority.

Peter's skepticism highlights the patriarchal attitudes that would later become entrenched in Christian orthodoxy. He questions why Jesus would choose to reveal such significant teachings to a woman, suggesting that her vision might be a fabrication. This dispute reflects broader historical struggles over the inclusion and recognition of women's spiritual contributions.

Levi's defense of Mary is crucial in the text. He rebukes Peter for his narrow-mindedness and acknowledges the validity of Mary's experience. Levi's support indicates that there were early Christian factions that recognized and valued the spiritual leadership of women. This acknowledgment of Mary's authority serves as a powerful statement about the inclusive and egalitarian nature of early Christian communities.

The Spiritual Message

The central message of the Gospel of Mary Magdalene revolves around the inner spiritual journey and the direct experience of the divine. It emphasizes personal revelation and the pursuit of gnosis, or knowledge, as the path to salvation. This approach contrasts with the emerging orthodoxy that placed greater emphasis on external authority and doctrinal conformity.

Mary's teachings stress the importance of overcoming ignorance and attachment to the material world. She encourages the disciples to look inward and cultivate a deep, personal connection with the divine. This inward focus is a key tenet of gnostic spirituality, which values inner transformation over external observance.

The gospel also highlights the transient nature of the material world and the eternal reality of the spiritual realm. Mary's vision underscores the soul's journey through various planes of existence, shedding earthly attachments and attaining higher states of consciousness. This cosmology reflects gnostic beliefs about the layered nature of reality and the soul's ultimate reunion with the divine source.

Modern Interpretation and Relevance

The Gospel of Mary Magdalene has gained renewed interest in contemporary times, particularly among scholars and spiritual seekers exploring alternative Christian traditions. Its portrayal of Mary as a prominent disciple and its emphasis on personal spiritual experience resonate with modern values of gender equality and individual autonomy.

For many, this gospel offers a vision of early Christianity that is more inclusive and spiritually dynamic than the hierarchical structures that later dominated the church. It provides a glimpse into a tradition where women played significant roles and where spiritual authority was based on personal insight rather than institutional position.

The text also invites modern readers to reflect on the nature of spiritual knowledge and the journey of the soul. Its teachings encourage a deeper exploration of inner consciousness and the pursuit of direct, transformative experiences of the divine. This emphasis on inner spirituality aligns with contemporary movements that seek to integrate ancient wisdom with modern spiritual practices.

The Gospel of Mary Magdalene is a powerful testament to the rich diversity of early Christian thought and the significant role of women in the early church. Its teachings on the nature of sin, the soul's journey, and the importance of personal spiritual experience offer valuable insights for contemporary spiritual seekers.

Through the figure of Mary Magdalene, this gospel challenges traditional narratives and opens up new possibilities for understanding the origins and evolution of Christian spirituality. It invites readers to consider a more inclusive and dynamic vision of the early Christian community, where spiritual authority is based on inner knowledge and personal transformation.

As interest in alternative Christian texts continues to grow, the Gospel of Mary Magdalene remains a vital and inspiring resource, offering a profound exploration of the inner journey and the quest for divine knowledge. Its message of inner transformation and spiritual empowerment resonates across the centuries, inviting each generation to embark on their own path of discovery and enlightenment.

End